IMAGES
of America

LINCOLN COUNTY

Beatrice Kovacs Mitchum
and Dianne Morgan Poteat

ARCADIA
PUBLISHING

ISBN 978-1-5316-6358-2

Published by Arcadia Publishing
Charleston, South Carolina

Library of Congress Control Number: 2012930192

For all general information, please contact Arcadia Publishing: Telephone
843-853-2070
Fax 843-853-0044
E-mail sales@arcadiapublishing.com
For customer service and orders:
Toll-Free 1-888-313-2665

Visit us on the Internet at www.arcadiapublishing.com

*Beatrice Kovacs Mitchum dedicates this work to her
husband, Eddy, for all that he has meant to her.*

*Dianne Morgan Poteat dedicates this work in memory of her
husband, Johnny, Mildred Estes Fortson, and Mary Lucy
Ware Probst for their impact and input in her life.*

CONTENTS

ACKNOWLEDGMENTS

The following people specifically made photographs, documents, and so on available to the authors for this work: Kenneth Adair, Wyatt B. and Nina Price Albea Jr., Robert M. Aycock, Virginia Aycock, Cynthia P. Balchin, Dimple Banks, Edwin Bentley, Dori Brown, Elizabeth Hardy Dallis, Brenda Turner Danner-McGahee, Vickie Dawkins, Gary Edwards, Charles Estes, Audrey Partridge Fleming, Elizabeth Spires Fleming, Nobie Dean Deason Hawes, Jacqueline Johnson, Nicole M. Kelley, Ann Mathews, John Cullars McCrimmon, Lamar and Helen McKinney, Dale Maddox, Jeannette Holloway Moragne, Lavina Glaze Marlow, Beth Drinkard Reed, Mamie Neil Spires Reed, Talmadge Reed Sr., Remmie Remsen, Dot Wellmaker Scott, Virginia Pugh Skinner, Maurice R. Spires, Edward and Lilly Holloway Turner, Jackie Poss Willingham, and William J. York Jr.

Those individuals, families, or estates that have donated family photographs, histories, original documents, and other information to the genealogical and historical archives of the Lincoln County Public Library are also integral to this project and must be thanked, including Dorothy Bentley, the Bohlers, Mitilda Bufford, William Bufford, the Cantelous, Emmye Ward Collins, Tom Elam, the Guillebeaus, the Hardys, Maggie Stidom Hogan, Shirley Hogan, the Lewis family, Mickie Macgee, Welcome and Rubye Mason, Ralph Martin, the McMahans, Mary Myers, the Nash family, Iris Norman, the Pinsons, the Praters, Mary Lucy Ware Probst, the Reids, the Sales, the Sims family, the Wards, the Wares, and the Wellmakers. There may be others we have missed, and we ask forgiveness for our oversight. Without the generosity of these individuals and families, this work would not exist. So much of what they offered could not fit within the confines of this work, and all items will become permanent resources available through the library's historical and genealogical programs.

We wish to thank Shirley Norman Dawkins, library director of the Lincoln County Public Library (LCPL), for her generosity in providing family photographs, time, sources, and most of all, for her moral support. Without her, this project would likely not have concluded. We owe her a debt that cannot be described. Also, we wish to thank John Cullars McCrimmon for his major contributions to the establishment of the John Cullars McCrimmon Genealogy Room, the computer lab, the circulation desk, and so on for the Lincoln County Public Library.

Finally, we must thank Elizabeth Bray and Liz Gurley, acquisitions editors for Arcadia Publishing, whose patience and helpfulness cannot be overstated.

The people of Lincoln County have been very positive about this project, and we must thank them. We also thank the *Lincoln Journal*, and its editor, Jacqueline Johnson, for providing permission to use materials that appeared in the newspaper.

INTRODUCTION

Lincoln County is a quiet gem in Georgia, with miles of freshwater coastline for recreation and scores of historical sites important to the history of the United States, including Revolutionary War and Civil War sites. It was created from the eastern portion of Wilkes County in 1796 and became a significant site during the American Revolution because of the rebels who hid in the forests. John Dooly, an important member of the militia, was captured and executed by Tories. Later, the Tory gang was caught and hanged near a pond now known as Tory Pond. Dooly's purported homesite is located near Elijah Clark State Park, named after another Revolutionary War officer, who also lived in Lincoln County. There is also Hester's Ferry State Park, named for a now defunct ferry service across the Broad River to Petersburg in Elbert County, Georgia, which was at one time the third-largest city in the state.

There were multiple ferry services traversing the Savannah and Broad Rivers from the 1700s that were discontinued only when Clarks Hill Dam (J. Strom Thurmond Dam) was built and Clarks Hill Lake was formed from 1946 to 1954. These ferries connected Lincoln County with Columbia and Elbert Counties, Georgia, and parts of Abbeville and Edgefield Counties, South Carolina, that in 1916 became McCormick County. Also, the Old Petersburg Road was one of the oldest roads connecting Augusta, Georgia, with the northern part of the state and ran through the county to Lisbon, once a thriving town in Lincoln County.

William Bartram, the famous naturalist, explored part of Lincoln County as he trekked on his Southern journey from March 1773 to January 1777. John Asbury, the famous Methodist circuit-riding preacher, came through the area and stayed at Bibbs Crossroads in the county; the exact location is still undiscovered.

During the Civil War, a large Confederate gold shipment was reported stolen during a sojourn at the Chennault Plantation in northern Lincoln County. It is also said that the gold Confederate seal was thrown into the Savannah River at Hester's ferry as the gold train crossed into Lincoln County accompanied by Jefferson Davis. The gold was never recovered. Hester's Ferry, now a popular campground and resort area near the homesite of the great Elijah Clark and family, was close to the area where the Confederate gold was rumored to be lost.

The early economy depended on farming, especially cotton and lumber, along with some tobacco. Farming continued to be the primary institution into the early 20th century. During the 1800s, there were several lumber mills and two ginneries. Cotton crop production decreased over the years, but lumber continues to be a major part of the economy.

Upheaval occurred in the 1940s when the US Army Corps of Engineers decided to build what is now called the J. Strom Thurmond Dam, damming the Savannah River and flooding the best of the farmland. Although tourism on the lake is now a major contributor to the local economy, it cannot match what was lost. Some records recently found include images of the homesites that were flooded in Lincoln County. Also, several extinct or current communities are not included in this book, such as Honora, Leathersville, Pansy, Kenna, Amity, Lockhart, Clay Hill, Agnes,

Woodlawn, and others due to space considerations. The only local mountain rising 900 feet above sea level, Graves Mountain is a major geological marvel, with quality gems and minerals, including amethyst, kyanite, hematite, sapphire, and other finds in the quarry.

The county and the city of Lincolnton have long histories of providing important people to serve in the military. Examples include Charles Estes, John Dooly, Elijah Clark, Andrew Jackson Reid, Aaron Hardy, John Cullars McCrimmon, and others.

There are records from the entire history of the county located in the courthouse, which provide a picture of life in this part of Georgia from the 1790s to the present day. These were accessed to describe lifestyles over 200 years. Focus is on the families of the county and their lives. Many locals agreed to share their family photographs and gave permission for their use.

Many people provided images for this work, but only a few could be used. Of over 800 donated images, no more than 240 were allowed. Therefore, parameters were set: no individual portraits except for military people, no houses or home places without families, and no multiple views of the same scene, place, or people if at all possible.

There is a poem called "Lincoln County," written by Bernice Legg for the 1923 Lincoln County Fair Association's Annual Exhibition. There is no room for the entire poem, but the first and last verses are below.

They asked me to write a poem
On the county we so much love;
On its farms, its homes and its people,
And its skies that smile above.

For the grandeur of country
Is not in its scenery fair;
But in the hearts and lives of people –
You will find its glory there.

One

LINCOLN COUNTY
TO 1900

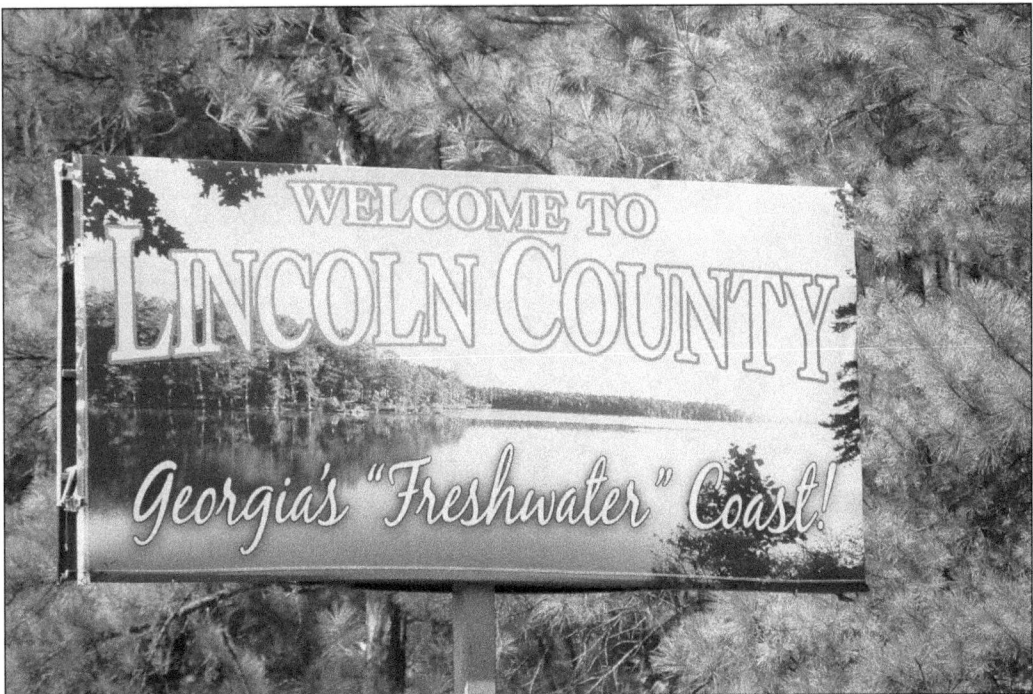

These billboards greet people entering Lincoln County from each direction on the major roadways. "'Freshwater Coast" refers to the many miles of lakeshore coast available for fishing, boating, and other water sports. (Photograph by Mitchum.)

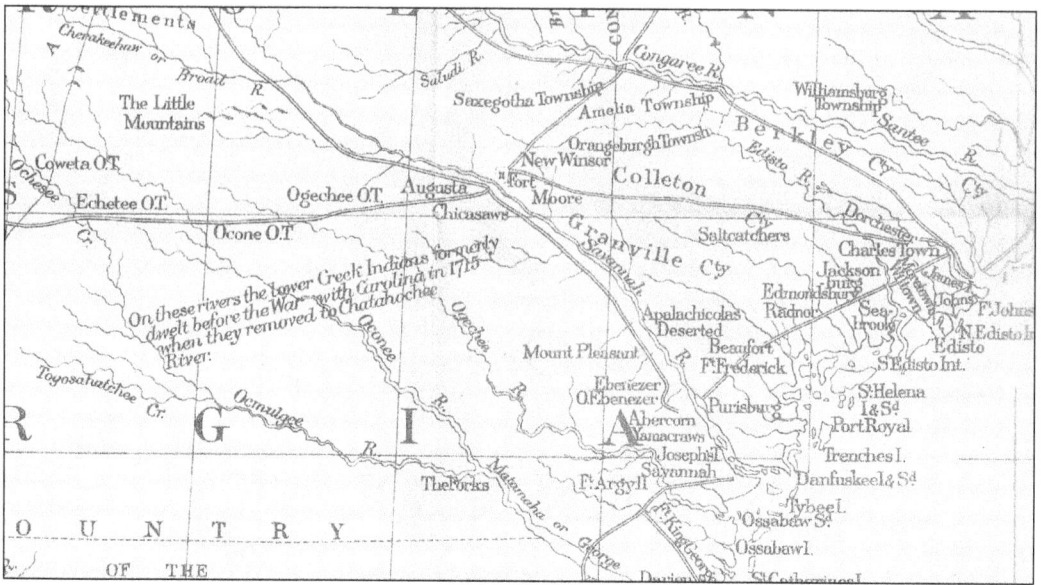

This is part of the Mitchell Map (1755), reproduced from plate No. 6 in *Early History of the Creek Indians and Their Neighbors* by John R. Swanton (Smithsonian Institution, Bureau of American Ethnology, Bulletin 73, 1922). It shows an area between Little River, Broad River, and the Savannah River that the local Indians called "the Little Mountains." It is now called Lincoln County, named for Benjamin Lincoln, who received the sword of Lord Cornwallis at the end of the American Revolution. (Courtesy of Mitchum.)

The Peter Lamar family cemetery sits in the heart of Lincolnton on Peachtree Street, within a short distance of "Founder's Spring." The Lamars founded Lincolnton, donating the land for the construction of the original town buildings. (LCPL.)

DEEP SOUTH REGION

WILLIAM BARTRAM TRAIL

TRACED 1773 - 1777

In 1775 took William Bartram north to Fort James on the "Petersburg Road" and passed through Lincoln County, parts now covered by Clark Hill Reservoir

ERECTED BY
Augusta Council of Garden Clubs, Inc.
IN COOPERATION WITH
Azalea District of the Garden Club of Georgia, Inc.
AND
U. S. Corp of Engineers

This historical marker identifies botanist William Bartram's trail as he traveled along the Georgia side of the Savannah River between 1773 and 1777, identifying plants in their habitats. His travels took him through Lincoln County. The marker is located at Wright's Crossing, at the intersection of Highways 378 and 43 (also known as Petersburg Road), which is the intersection located in front of the Wright house. (LCPL.)

William Bartram was a naturalist who identified plants in their habitats during the 18th century. His portrait includes a small flower that extrudes from a buttonhole in his vest. (LCPL.)

Located in the Elijah Clark State Park, the Elijah Clark House is a replica of the original log cabin used by his family. The park, open year-round, has many attractions for visitors and locals alike. In the fall, there is a bluegrass festival over a weekend, drawing talent from around the country. The park also has fishing tournaments and cabins for rent, along with multiple campgrounds for both tent and motor home camping. (Photograph by Mathews.)

Having a detached kitchen outside the house reduced fire hazards. Therefore, this design was common during the early days, with cooking being done away from the house and brought in by servants. (Photograph by Mathews.)

Gen. Elijah Clark was born in Edgecombe County, North Carolina, in 1733 and moved to what was then a part of Wilkes County, Georgia, in 1774. When the Revolutionary War began, he joined the militia and became a colonel. Clark led the patriots against the British in battles at various creeks and two sieges at Augusta, using tactics that earned him the nickname "Hero of Hornet's Nest." (LCPL.)

Elijah Clark's tombstone, located in Elijah Clark State Park, identifies the reinterred remains of General Clark and those of his family that were moved before Clarks Hill Lake inundated the cemetery sites. They were previously buried near Graball, which is 10 miles north of Lincolnton. (Photograph by Mitchum.)

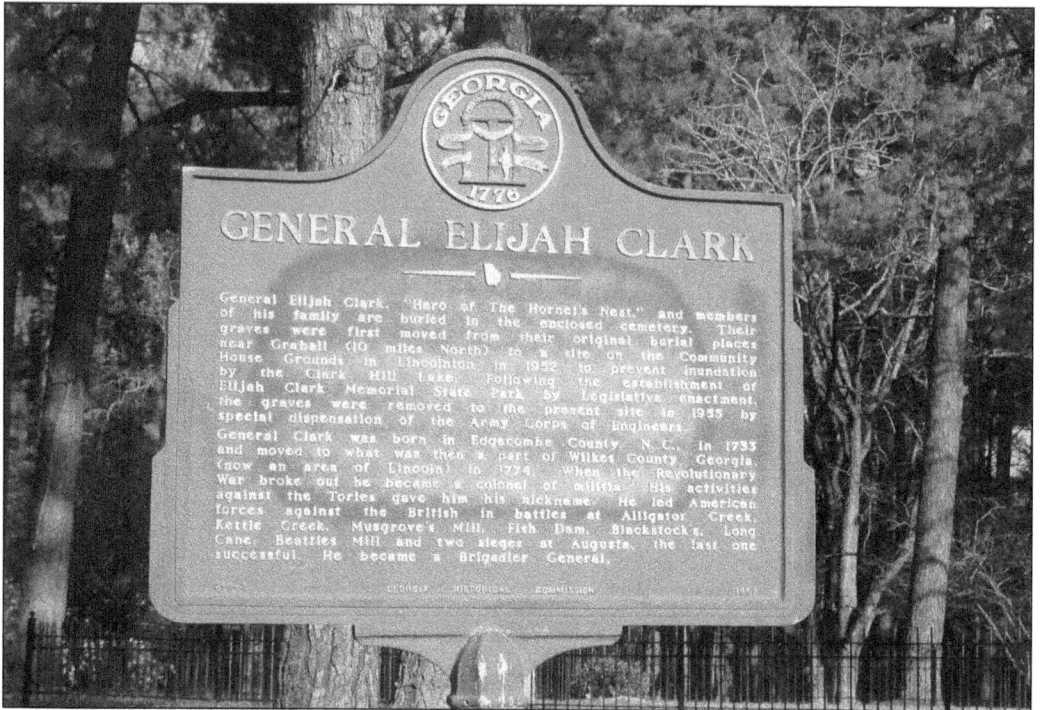

This Gen. Elijah Clark historical marker describes how the Hero of Hornet's Nest and family were moved and the significant military action he saw during the 1700s. (Photograph by Mitchum.)

After Lincoln County was formed in 1796, only one town existed within its boundaries, Lisbon. It was located at the confluence of the Savannah and Broad Rivers. Men were appointed to find a central location for a county seat and public domain. Peter Lamar's land, with a plentiful water supply (because he dammed a spring), was chosen. The Lamar family deeded three acres encompassing the spring for the town, fittingly named Lincolnton. The spring is known as "Founder's Spring." (Photograph by Mathews.)

During the Revolutionary War, this tavern, known as the Guillebeau Inn, had a prison below the main floor where the Tories who were responsible for the assassination of Revolutionary War patriot Col. John Dooly were held overnight until they were hanged and burned. Later, the building was used as a school, then a hotel, and finally a dwelling, owned by the Guillebeau family. Sadly, it was destroyed by fire in September 1972. (Courtesy of Nina Albea.)

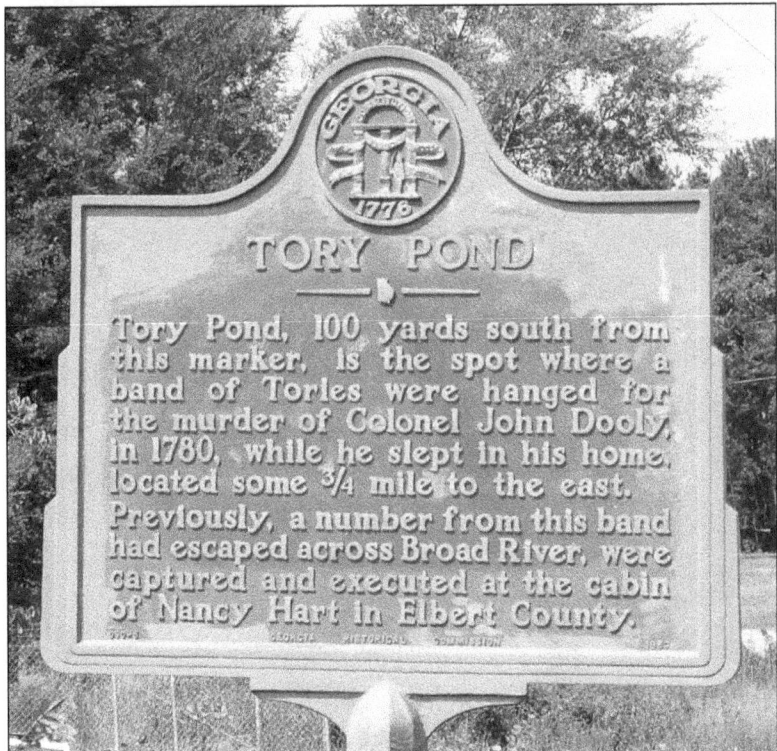

Tory Pond, located off US Highway 378 east of Lincolnton and near Elijah Clark State Park, was the site of the hanging of a band of Tories for the murder of Col. John Dooly in 1780 while he slept in his cabin. Previously, a number of this band had escaped across Broad River to the north. They were captured by Nancy Hart and executed at her cabin in Elbert County. (Photograph by Mitchum.)

Dooly Spring is to the left of this marker and was used by the John Dooly family. They had a simple log cabin across the road opposite the spring. It was here that Tories murdered Col. John Dooly during the Revolutionary War. (Photograph by Mitchum.)

On March 17, 2002, the National Society Daughters of the American Revolution honored the graves of Hezekiah Bussey and Zachariah Spiers in the St. Paul United Methodist Church graveyard. Bussey followed General Clark into the Battle of Kettle Creek that turned the tide in favor of the Patriots and was recognized as a Revolutionary War soldier. Spiers contributed to the army of Gen. Nathaniel Greene in South Carolina and was designated a Revolutionary War patriot. (Photograph by Mitchum.)

Hollingshead-Hogan blacksmith shop is a replica of the old blacksmith shop on the Augusta Highway. It contains two forges, one run with bellows and the other with a hand-turned blower. Numerous tools and artifacts have been acquired, including blacksmith anvils, forges, and other tools as well as horseshoes and pieces of harness. At the annual Pioneer Day held on the Saturday before Thanksgiving in the Lincoln County Historical Park, volunteer blacksmiths demonstrate their art. (Photograph by Mitchum.)

Records show that Andrew Jackson Reid once lived in this house built in the 1800s. Reid fought for the South in the Civil War, was captured at Gettysburg in 1863, and was released and returned home in 1865. Dr. Robert Williams donated the cabin to the Lincoln County Historical Society. (Photograph by Mitchum.)

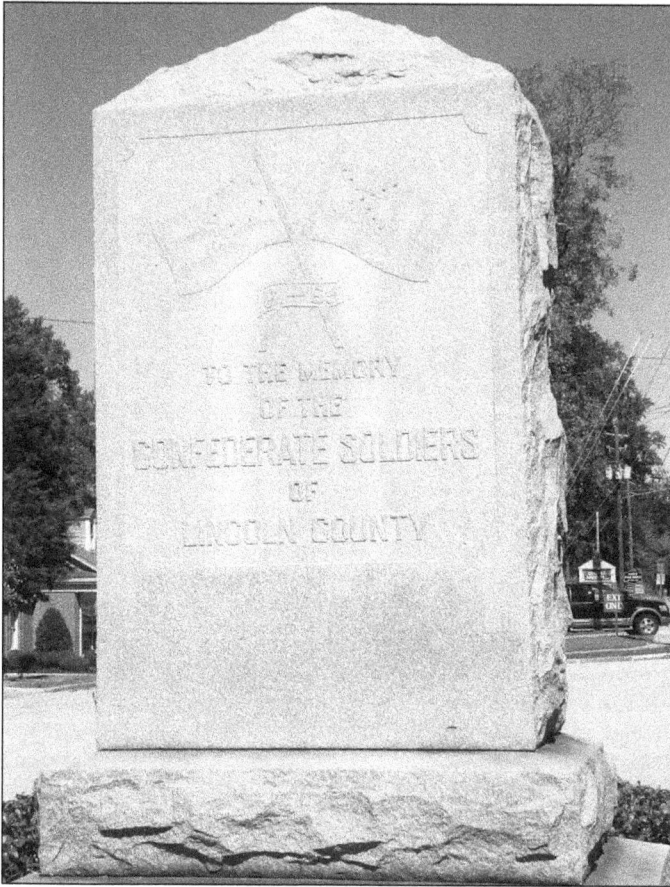

The Daughters of the Confederacy erected this monument in 1918, memorializing Lincoln County's contribution to the Confederate war effort. Several Georgia regiments were organized with Lincoln County soldiers. The monument marks the original town square and the site of the first courthouse in Lincolnton. (Photograph by Mitchum.)

This view of Peachtree Street looks eastward, and in the distance is the bell tower of the Lincolnton United Methodist Church. The first bank in the town, the Bank of Lincolnton, is on the right, with the original Crawford Drugstore next to it. The white frame building on the left was Blanchard Wright's grocery store. The men are unidentified, and it is thought that this was taken in the late 1800s. (LCPL.)

On the steps of the Wright house at Wright's Crossing are the members of the Marshall William and Nancy Jane Starke Wright family. The children's names are Robert Marshall, Martha Leona "Mattie," Otis Benjamin, Mary Jane, and Gladys. (LCPL.)

This building served as the kitchen for the Wright house on US Highway 378 and Petersburg Road, east of Lincolnton. With a breezeway connecting it to the house, the kitchen was in use until 1973. (Photograph by Mitchum.)

The Wellmaker family portrait shows, from left to right, (second row) Alvin, father; Clyde Wellmaker, and Betty Jones, mother; (first row) Lydia Mitchell Wellmaker (Paradise), Eli "Bud," and Suzanna Wellmaker (Goldman). (Courtesy of Dot Scott.)

This photograph was taken at the old Bohler home located on Tankersley Road. Family members include, from left to right, (from left) Babe, Willard, Winnie, Ernest W., Agnes, Lloyd, Olin Moncrief, Pete, Buddy, Talmadge, Bill Gassaway, Pat Gassaway, Jeffrey Leeward, Wes, and Emmy. (Courtesy of Jeannette Moragne.)

This is the Ivey family and their home place in Iveytown. Unfortunately, the family's names have been lost. (Courtesy of Lilly Turner.)

Burgess home place is shown around 1895, with most of the family in front. Those pictured are, from left to right, Jabez West Burgess, William Thomas Burgess, Groves Burgess (Will's son), Dora Burgess, Lena Burgess (Charles's daughter), Charles Brantley Burgess, Frank Burgess, Martha Banks Burgess (wife of Rev. Pleasant Frank Burgess), Robert L. Burgess, and Nellie Burgess (Charles's daughter). The reverend is the only member missing from this photograph. (Courtesy of Jeannette Moragne.)

Confederate soldier Thomas Lewis Ware (1838–July 2, 1863) was killed at the Battle of Gettysburg. His diary and the diary of a Union soldier were the subjects of a book about the Civil War written by Mark Nesbitt called *35 Days to Gettysburg*. (Courtesy of Dianne M. Poteat.)

Walter Murray Remsen, second from right, poses with members of the 2nd Georgia Volunteer Infantry during the Spanish-American War on May 10, 1898, in Griffin, Georgia. (LCPL.)

Two

MILITARY SINCE 1900

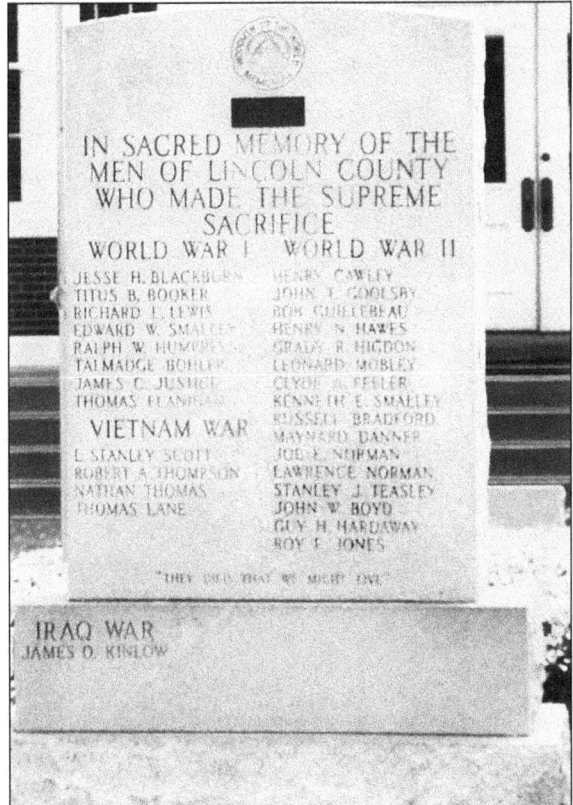

War Memorial monument in front of the Lincoln County Courthouse states, "In Memory of the Men Of Lincoln County Who Made the Supreme Sacrifice." Names are listed of those who perished in World War I, World War II, the Vietnam War, and the Iraq War. (Photograph by Mitchum.)

Clarence Edgar Freeland (1881–1961) was the first-born of Walter B. and Mary "Minnie" Musgrove Freeland. He served as a first lieutenant in the Quartermaster Corps in World War I. (LCPL.)

Seaborn "Seeb" Jones served in the Army in World War I and is seen here with an unidentified friend. He was married to Izzie Dora Goldman and was a well-respected member of the Mountain community of Lincoln County. (Courtesy of Dot Scott.)

Nathan Mason of Lincoln County served during World War I. Once he left the service, it is said that he decided to leave the county and moved to Cleveland, Ohio, where he lived out the rest of his life. He was an uncle of Welcome Mason, a highly respected member of the county. (Courtesy of Welcome and Rubye Mason.)

William Jackson Scott Sr. served in the Army Medical Corps during World War I. He was the husband of Fannie May Tullis Scott, and they had one daughter and three sons. He died in 1957. (Courtesy of Dot Scott.)

Boyd Maynard Aycock Jr. (1919–2004) poses for his Army photograph. He lived near Graves Mountain, married Edith McKinney, and managed the Aycock Brothers Lumber Company. Boyd took many of the photographs donated by his son Robert "Bobby" Aycock that appear in this book. (Courtesy of Bobby Aycock.)

Harold Bunch of Lincoln County stands on his PT boat in the Pacific in 1943–1944. (Courtesy of Billy York.)

Leslie (left) and Welcome Holloway stand on the Little River Bridge in 1942. (Courtesy of Jeannette Moragne.)

Pictured here are, from left to right, (first row) Frances Norman Bryan and Clarence Edward Norman; (second row) Mary Sallie Bentley Norman, William Peyton Norman, and Peyton William Norman. (Courtesy of Iris Norman and LCPL.)

Thomas Parks (1910–1985) served in the US Army during World War II. He was a farmer and served on the executive committee of the Georgia Baptist Association. (Courtesy of Jackie Willingham.)

Burrel Poss (left), Pete Dunnefin, and Lucy Cartledge stand in front of the Estes house and the Myers house in the 1940s. (Courtesy of Jackie Willingham.)

Will Tom Jones served during World War II. When his parents died, the children were distributed to other families. The family of local physician Dr. William Henry Estes raised his brother Percy, and the Mason family raised Will Tom. (Courtesy of Welcome and Rubye Mason.)

Dorothy Ellen Partridge, in her Navy uniform, stands in front of Lincolnton High School on May 25, 1945. She was the daughter of William Sidney Partridge Sr. and Mary Emma Freeland Partridge. She retired after serving her country honorably for 30 years in the US Navy. (Courtesy of Audrey Partridge Fleming.)

The Thomas Watson and Kate Rumbley Reese family gather around 1943 during World War II. Those pictured include, from left to right, Walter Holloway (raised by the Reeses), Thomas Watson (back), Kate Rumbley, Thomas "T.W." Watson Jr., Sara Reese Guillebeau, Sudie Reese Holloway, Marvin ?, and Lena Reese Cliatt. The child is unidentified. (Courtesy of Jeannette Moragne.)

Leonard Stanley Scott Sr. during World War II served as a staff sergeant who trained troops in the United States. He was married to Dorothy Wellmaker Scott, and they had two sons and one daughter. (Courtesy of Dot Scott.)

William Jackson "Jack" Scott Jr. (born 1924) served in the Navy during World War II. He is the son of William Jackson Scott Sr. and Frances Mae Tullis. (Courtesy of Dot Scott.)

On the left is Lt. Col. William Jesse York Sr. of the 15th Tank Battalion, 6th Army Division in Belgium during World War II. He was married to Doris Bunch York, had graduated from North Georgia College, and served in Japan, Germany, and France. He earned a Bronze Star, Purple Heart, Army Commendation Medal, and other medals. (Courtesy of Billy York.)

Leonard Summers served during World War II. There is little information about him available. (Courtesy of Cynthia Balchin.)

MSgt. John Cullars McCrimmon (left), shown in a bunker in Korea with Private Cox, served in the Army during three wars—World War II, Korea, and Vietnam—and retired at the rank of master sergeant. During his service, he received multiple awards of the Combat Infantryman Badge, Purple Hearts, and other commendations for his service. He is a major benefactor of the historical, genealogical, and computer resources of the Lincoln County Public Library. (Courtesy of John McCrimmon.)

Billy Bunch (second row, second from left), a World War II Navy veteran, is shown in this photograph with his minesweeper crew. (Courtesy of Billy York.)

A Lincoln County contingent meets up at Sheppard Air Force Base in Wichita Falls, Kansas, in 1952. They are, from left to right, Calvin Lewis, Billy Norman, Bobby Moss, and Carleton Beggs. (Courtesy of Billy Norman.)

Theron Coombs Price relaxes on the battleship *Arizona* before it was sunk at Pearl Harbor on December 7, 1941. He was married to Frances Marie Albea, had one daughter, and died in 1987. For many years, he drove a school bus in the county and, after the death of his father, he ran Price's store in the Double Branches community. (Courtesy of Nina Albea.)

William Sheldon Kelley served in the US Army in Vietnam. He also served in the US Air Force during the Korean War. (Courtesy of Nichole Kelley.)

Billy York relaxes in a jeep in Vietnam while serving in the Army. He is a graduate of North Georgia College. (Courtesy of Billy York.)

Bobby Aycock's identification photograph shows that he was in the Air Force in 1963. He is the son of Boyd and Edith McKinney Aycock. (Courtesy of Bobby Aycock.)

This elegant tombstone reads, "Titus B. Booker / Born June 23, 1892 / Died Sept. 30, 1918 / Age 26 yrs. 3 mos. 7 days / He left his home in / perfect health. He looked / so young and brave. / We little thought / how soon he'd be / laid in a soldier's grave." (Photograph by Mitchum.)

Leonard Stanley Scott Jr. was the son of Leonard Stanley Scott Sr. and Dorothy Wellmaker Scott. Shortly after his marriage to Shirley Arnett, he was drafted into the US Army. He was killed during the Vietnam War. He, too, "looked so young and brave." (Courtesy of Dot Scott.)

Three

CLARKS HILL LAKE

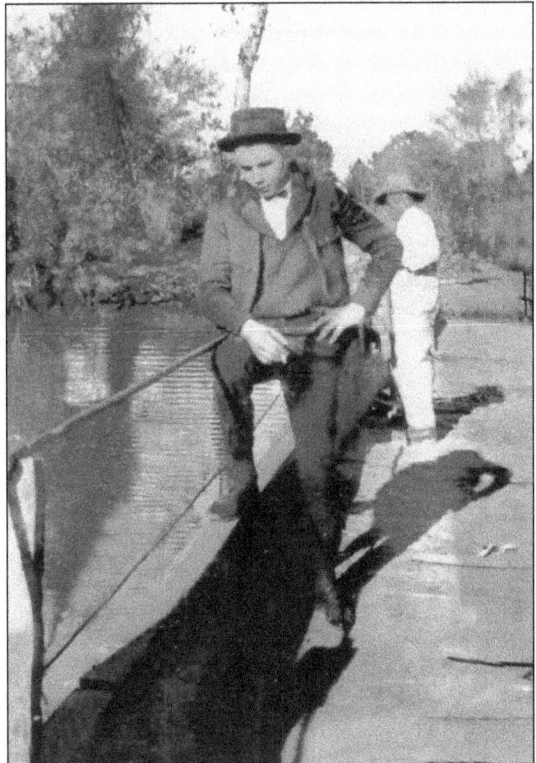

The Chamberlain Ferry, downriver from Lisbon, Georgia, connected Lincoln County with McCormick, South Carolina. Today, Chamberlain Ferry Road in Lincoln County, starting at Augusta Road (GA 47), runs into Clarks Hill Lake, and on the South Carolina side, the remainder of Chamberlain Ferry Road continues out of the water to end at US Highway 378, west of McCormick. The men are unidentified. (Courtesy of Jeannette Moragne.)

Fortson Ferry operated between Lincoln County and what is now McCormick County, South Carolina. Ben Fortson, early owner of this ferry service, died while trying to save his drowning ferryman. (Courtesy of Nina Albea.)

The Moseley Ward family enjoys fishing from one of the many ferries that once crossed the Savannah River. In this picture, one can gauge the width of the Savannah River between Lincoln County and McCormick County, South Carolina. (LCPL.)

The Lisbon Ferry connected the Old Petersburg Road at Lisbon with Petersburg, in Elbert County, at the junction of the Savannah and Broad Rivers. Major trade routes had to use ferries to cross these rivers because there were few bridges during the early years of the county. (Courtesy of Charles Estes.)

Lisbon Ferry on Petersburg Road ran between Lincoln and Elbert Counties until January 1952. Wilson Edwards and his wife operated the ferry. A bridge was to be built to take its place, but was never completed, causing hardship for the locals. (LCPL.)

Price's Bridge, before the Clarks Hill Dam, spanned the Little River between Lincoln and Columbia Counties. When asked about the "wooden bridge," the ones that remember always open their eyes wide, inhale a gulp of air, and say, "Yessiree, it was a long way to the bottom." (LCPL.)

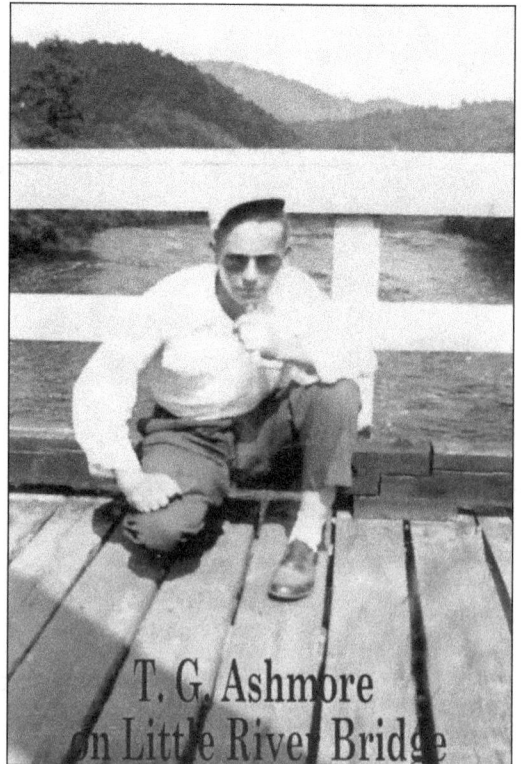

T. G. Ashmore on Little River Bridge

This photograph of T.G. Ashmore on the Little River Bridge shows some of the terrain in the background in the 1940s. (Courtesy of Jeannette Moragne.)

As the plans went forward for building the Clarks Hill Dam, engineers began constructing the Price-Legg Bridge over Little River in the 1940s. This bridge is a major north-south thoroughfare between Columbia and Lincoln Counties. (Courtesy of Kenneth Adair.)

This view of Fishing Creek was taken during the drought in 2011. It clearly shows what would normally be flooded along with the original creek channel. In the early days of the county, most people settled next to a source of water, such as this creek, along with Soap Creek, the Savannah River, Little River, and the Broad River. Many of these early homes were destroyed when the lake filled. (LCPL.)

At the start of the dam-
building project, the US Army
Corps of Engineers created
an overlook for sightseers.
The sign above the lookout
area reads, "Clarks Hill Dam,"
and was erected in May 1948.
(Courtesy of Bobby Aycock.)

Bobby Aycock mugs for the
camera while earthmovers
work diligently in the
distance leveling the ground
for the construction of the
Clarks Hill Dam. (Courtesy
of Bobby Aycock.)

The sign at the side of the road overlooking the construction of the Clarks Hill Dam says, "Construction Area. DANGER. Visitors not allowed beyond this point. Corps of Engineers War Dept." (Courtesy of Bobby Aycock.)

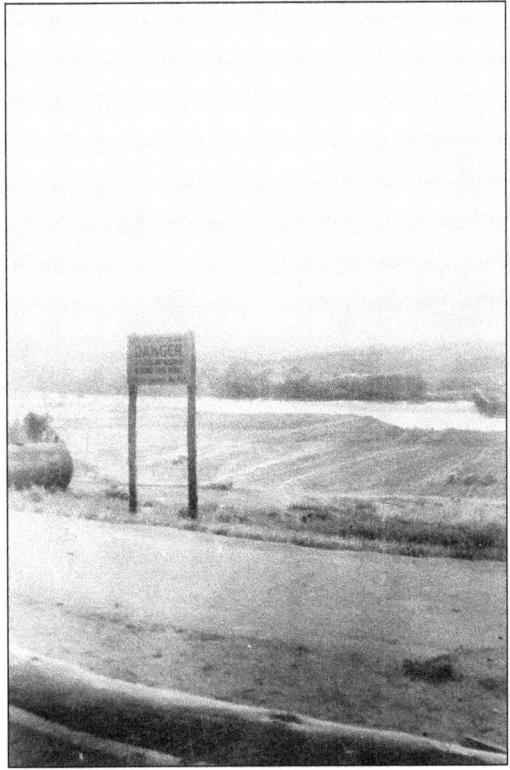

Here, the lake starts to fill after the dam is completed, and Lincoln County farmland starts to disappear. The lake continued to fill for the next several years. (Courtesy of Bobby Aycock.)

This is the bridge over the Savannah River and Clarks Hill Lake, located on US Highway 378 between Lincoln County, Georgia, and McCormick, South Carolina, that was built when the lake filled and ferries were no longer viable. Construction on a new replacement bridge began in 2011 and is expected to be complete in 2013. (Courtesy of Bobby Aycock.)

Ilean Cooper Martin poses on the newly completed US Highway 378 bridge, named the Fortson-Dorn Bridge, in the 1950s. (Courtesy of Jackie Willingham.)

The Wilson Edwards store, located in Lisbon, Georgia, is shown prior to inundation by Clarks Hill Lake. (Courtesy of Kenneth Adair.)

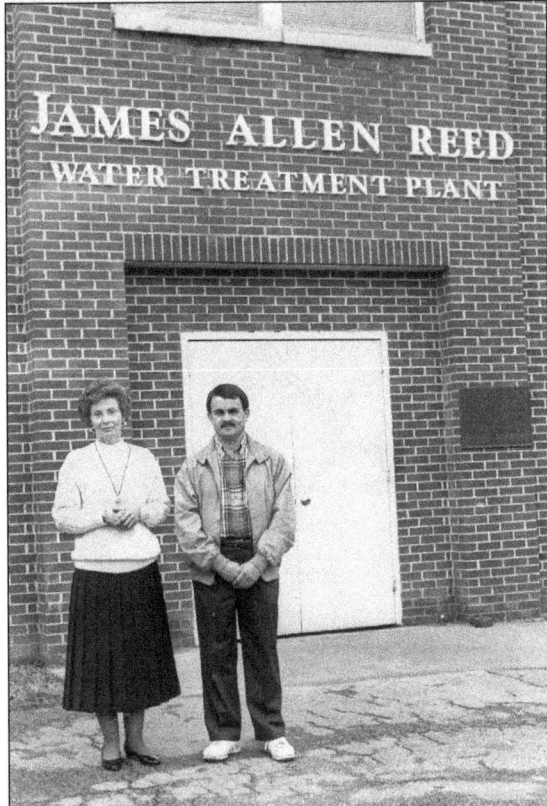

The first superintendent of the water department, James Allen Reed, who was a US Army veteran of the Korean War, died in July 1993. Shortly after his death, the water treatment plant on US Highway 378 was renamed in his honor. In front of the building are his widow, Mamie Neil Spires Reed, and Lincolnton mayor Lee Moss. (Courtesy of Mamie Neil Reed.).

Clarks Hill Dam, pictured here from the Georgia side, was renamed the J. Strom Thurmond Dam in South Carolina but remains Clarks Hill (both the lake and the dam) on the Georgia side. This photograph was taken in 2002. (Photograph by Mitchum.)

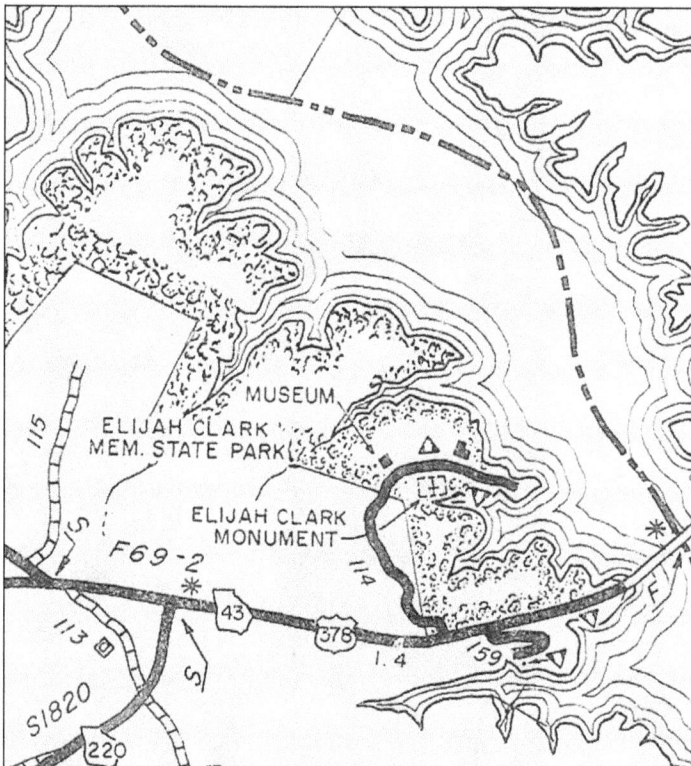

The Elijah Clark State Park was the first state park opened by the US Army Corps of Engineers after the Clarks Hill Lake filled and was dedicated the 1950s. The dotted line on the right shows the main channel (once the Savannah River bed), with US Highway 378 at the bottom and part of the Fortson-Dorn Bridge on the lower right. (LCPL.)

Four

PARKS, RECREATION, AND SPORTS

Cherokee Park, named for nearby Cherokee Creek, is popular with anglers and has a picnic area with this pavilion, fish cleaning stations, and so on. Located near the Price-Legg Bridge, it sports one of the longest boat ramps on the lake. Once a state-managed park, Cherokee is now managed by Lincoln County. (Photograph by Mitchum.)

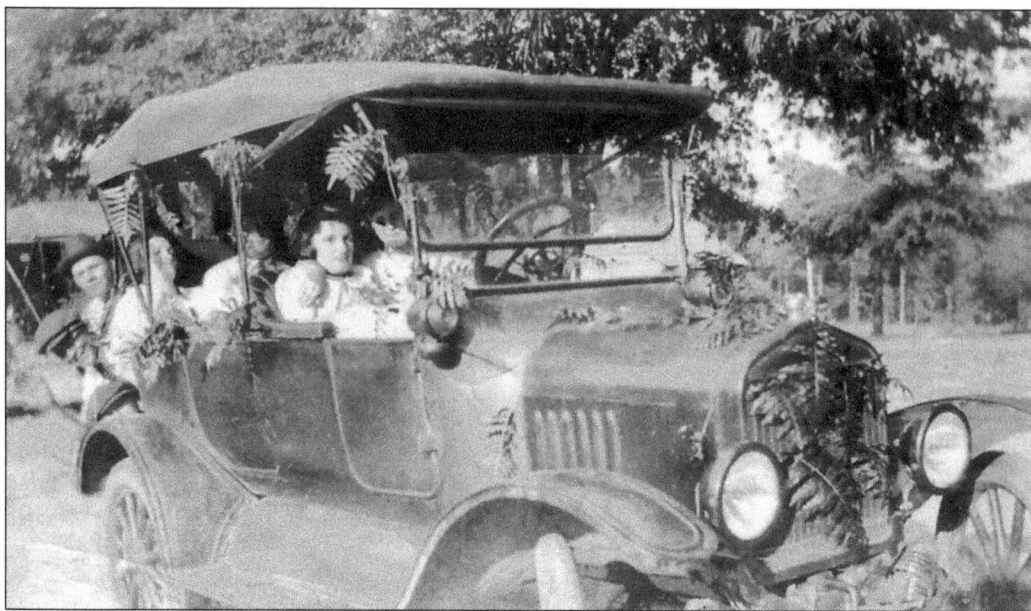

The photograph of this fern-covered car was taken in the early 1910s or 1920s. It is unknown whether this vehicle was decorated for a parade—or driven by a particularly thrill-seeking driver. (Courtesy of Bobby Aycock.)

While these women are unidentified, many Lincoln County residents picnicked in the countryside. Judging by the model of the car, this outing occurred during the 1940s. (Courtesy of Bobby Aycock.)

This item appears in the *Lincoln Journal*, identifying many important members of the Lincoln County community who are posing in this shot in 1914. The photograph includes, from left to right, Doc Pigue, A.M. Moore, Doc Reese, Morgan Holloway, John Silvey, Ed Miller, Bob Ashmore, Marion Holloway, A.M. "Bud" Holloway, Dick Ashmore, Ellis Holloway, Alf Dunn, and Alf Moore Jr. In the background, a baseball team is warming up. (Courtesy of Vickie Dawkins.)

With Graves Mountain in the background, these two unidentified fellows are showing off for the camera. Behind them, men are playing baseball. This was probably taken in the late 1940s. (Courtesy of Bobby Aycock.)

James Thomas Sale (1906–1987) is trying his luck at catching supper on Clarks Hill Lake. He and his wife, Iris Nash Sale, opened their home as a bed-and-breakfast on US Highway 378 in the Lincolnton city limits. (LCPL.)

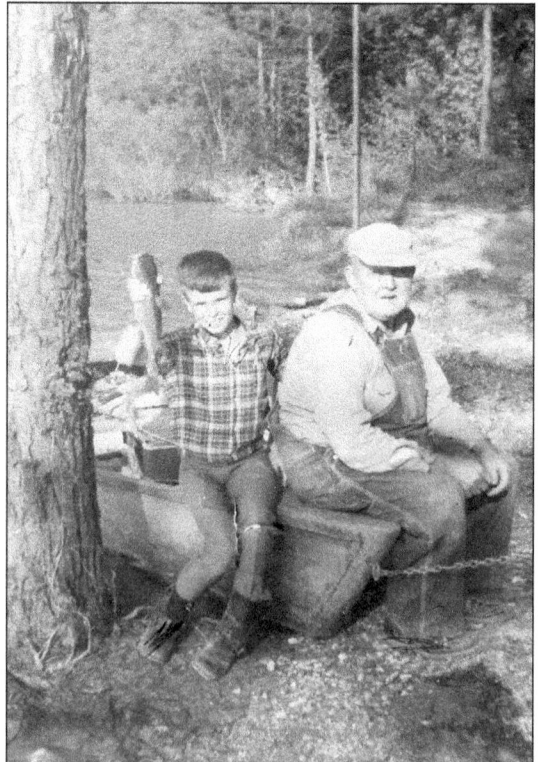

Chris Holloway (left) and Leeward Bohler enjoy one of the major sports in Lincoln County, fishing. (Courtesy of Jeannette Moragne.)

While serving in the US Navy, Dorothy Partridge earned fame as "the Georgia Pitch"er of the National Women's Softball League's Chicago Bloomer Girls in 1946. (Courtesy of Audrey Partridge Fleming.)

FLEET SERVICE DIVISION
nominates
Dorothy PARTRIDGE
SK2 (W)
The GEORGIA "PITCH"er
USN

PLAYED PROFESSIONAL SOFTBALL FOR THE NATIONALLY FAMOUS CHICAGO BLOOMER GIRLS OF THE NATIONAL WOMEN'S SOFTBALL LEAGUE IN 1946. SHE HAS ALSO DONNED UNIFORMS OF TWO OTHER CHICAGO PRO CLUBS--THE CHICKS AND THE CARDINALS.

MEMBER OF CHAMPIONSHIP TEAMS THAT COPPED THE STATE TITLE IN BOTH BASKETBALL AND SOFTBALL DURING 1944 THRU 1946 WHILE AT NSC OAKLAND

MOUND MAINSTAY OF THE R.H. WAVES IN THIS YEAR'S 49th STATE INVITATIONAL WOMEN'S SOFTBALL LEAGUE

AWARDED MOST VALUABLE AND OUTSTANDING PLAYER TROPHY WHEN SHE PITCHED A LOCAL SOFTBALL TEAM TO FIRST PLACE

Rocky Branch Golf Course is the only course in the county. It is located across the road from the old Watkins Chapel Church site on Double Branches Road. (Photograph by Mitchum.)

Lewis Family Pavilion, located in the Lincoln County Historical Park, was constructed in 2001 and named in honor of the Lewis family of Lincolnton, Georgia, in 2003. The pavilion is available for use by groups and organizations. (Photograph by Mitchum.)

Perched on the side of Soap Creek (part of Clarks Hill Lake) is Soap Creek Restaurant, famed for its seafood and country atmosphere. People travel as much as an hour or more just to have supper there. (Photograph by Mitchum.)

This article from the *Lincoln Journal* features the Lincolnton High School's track team in 1922. Pictured are, from left to right, (second row) coach H.D. Breazeale, Ben "Dick" Cliatt, Allen Hardy, Frank Sims, and principal J.E. Guillebeau; (first row) Charles Scott, R.T. Lewis, and Manley Clary. (LCPL.)

PERHAPS LHS'S FIRST TRACK TEAM – 1922

Seated, l-r, Charles Scott, R. T. Lewis, Manley Clary. Standing; l-r, Coach H. D. Breazeale, Ben "Dick" Cliatt, Allan Hardy, Frank Sims, and J. E. Guillebeau, principal.   —Photo submitted by Dick Cliatt

Pictured is the 1928 Lincolnton High School girls' basketball team. Members are, from left to right, Myrtle Keeter, Mildred Penland, Cleo Keeter, Lucille Lois Smith, Vivian Hogan, Mae Estes, Louise Bunch, and Kathleen Gresham. (LCPL.)

Lincolnton High School's 1937 football team, with the school in the background, includes, from left to right, (first row) Thomas Paradise, Emory Flint, John May, Neal Wansley, James "Jip" Smalley, and Bob Guillebeau; (second row) Clayton Myers, Irwin "Bud" Moss, coach Rollins Jones, Kelly Mims, Tommy Cunningham, and Billy Bunch. (LCPL.)

Pictured here is the 1940 Lincolnton High School football team. From left to right are (first row) Eddie Martin, Curry Colvin, C.G. Smalley, and Cluese Fleming; (second row) Charles Teasley, Jerry Groves, Basking Brown, Langley Norman, Pat Elam, Billy McWhorter, and Harris Denham; (third row) Alex Dunaway, Melvin Timmerman, and Charles Elam, (fourth row), Tom Boyd (teacher), Leonard Scott, Lester Reed, Jack Boyd, Jack Davis, Kenneth Goolsby, Eugene Graves, and Jim Boyd. (LCPL.)

54

The 1954 Lincolnton High School baseball team includes, from left to right, (first row) Jimmie Goldman, Allen Wells, Sonny Wall, Sting Dawkins, Bill Odom, and James "Buggy" Smith; (second row) Charles Hahn, J.R. Scott, Bill Snider, George Wesley Ware, Charles Ware, and Alex Willingham. (LCPL.)

The 1954–1955 Lincolnton High School cheerleaders pose in front of the school. From left to right are Carolyn Stephenson (Link), Lavina Glaze (Marlow), Beth Drinkard (Reed), Glenda Reed (Hines), Jackie Banks (Adams), Frankie Glaze (Phillips), Jean Lankston, and Carol McGee (Swift). (Courtesy of Beth Reed.)

This shot of the Lincoln County High School football team was taken in 1959, with coach Buddy Bufford. (Courtesy of Billy York.)

This is a view of the valley from Graves Mountain; the scene was obliterated when quarrying began on the mountain. The three-gabled house in the middle of the view is the Kinney-McKinney home place, which is no longer in existence. (Courtesy of Bobby Aycock.)

Here, Joe Cox and Kate Parks are spending time on Graves Mountain, a popular "date spot." This was probably taken in the 1930s. (Courtesy of Jackie Willingham.)

In the mid-1940s, Edith McKinney (Aycock) perches atop Graves Mountain with a shotgun. Lover's Leap is "where," the gun is "what," and the question that remains is "why?" (Courtesy of Bobby Aycock.)

Lessie Mae S. (left), Leland Frazier (second from left), Irene Powell, and Ingrahm Ward enjoy an outing on Graves Mountain; the date is unknown. (LCPL.)

Here, Idys (left) and Susie LeRoy are shown on Graves Mountain; the date of the photograph is unknown. The LeRoy family migrated to Lincoln County from the French Huguenot settlement of New Bordeaux, South Carolina. (LCPL.)

George Kinney and grandson
Carleton McKinney stand at the
mouth of "Wolf's Den" at Graves
Mountain sometime in the 1940s.
This popular cave was destroyed when
quarrying operations began. Carleton
was the son of Horace Herman
and Rosalie Kinney McKinney.
(Courtesy of Bobby Aycock.)

Newt Pinson Sr. is looking out over
the valley from Graves Mountain.
This view is no longer available
because the rock and 150 feet of
the mountaintop were removed by
the mining operation. (LCPL.)

The quarry at Graves Mountain removed Lover's Leap, Wolf's Den, and a large portion of the mountain along with some of the home places in the valley. This photograph, taken in 2010, shows the quarry that is open two weekends each year (spring and fall) for the public to explore the wealth of minerals without charge. For current year opening dates, search the Internet for "Graves Mountain Georgia." (Photograph by Mitchum.)

Elizabeth "Lib" Estes (left) and Denise Reese Burton Hamrick pose with the Lincolnton Club House sign. The clubhouse was built in the 1930s by Cleon Prince, purported to be the "only person in Lincoln County who could read blueprints" at that time, with the assistance of the Civilian Conservation Corps. (LCPL.)

Five

SCHOOLS

This distinguished gentleman is Dr. C.V.A. Grier. He was named Vera Cruz Abdalonumus Grier but he changed the sequence of the initials "in the interest of euphony." He was born in 1866, started teaching in 1879, and studied languages, including Latin, Greek, and Hebrew (in which he read the Bible). He lived in a small cabin with his wife and his dogs and a cat. "Uncle Grier" was known as one of the "best-educated" men in this section of the nation. He passed his teacher examination at the age of 11. He lived in the Agnes community and walked 26 miles round-trip to Double Branches to teach school. He taught for 68 years in Lincoln County. (LCPL.)

Amity School, added to the National Register of Historic Places in 1993, was a school and then a social meeting place. It was built in 1900, and this photograph was probably taken sometime before 1915. It still serves as a community center for Woodlawn, Clay Hill, Amity, and surrounding areas. (LCPL.)

ANTHONY'S CHAPEL SCHOOL PUPILS 1907 OR 1908

FRONT ROW, left to right, Henry Ware, W. C. Allgood, Net Ware, Pharris Stribling, Willie Ware, Lucile Walton, (Unidentified), Lizzie Henderson, Celeste Standard, Minnie Lee Henderson, Charlie Walton, Louise Wheatley, Wayne Brown, Ella Brown, Clara Wheatley, Duncan Ware, Harvey Wheatley.

SECOND ROW, left to right, Pete Henderson, Cecil Henderson, Albert Wheatley, Janie Brown, Nettie Wheatley, Lora Wheatley, Miss

Pearl Kirkland, teacher, Susie Stribling, B Ogletree , Boyce Standard, Joe Powell, Estelle Wheatley, Hoyt Allgood.

BACK ROW, left to right, Brantley Wheatley, Grover Wheatley, L. M. Brown, Lizzie Powell, Effie Brown, Blanche Ware, Lillie Brown, Rosa Mae Wheatley, Margaret Owens, Sweet Johnson, Branham Ware, Leonard Wheatley, (Unidentified)
—Photo submitted by Mrs. Celeste Standard Brown

This photograph of Anthony's Chapel School is from the *Lincoln Journal* and shows students during the 1907 or 1908 school year. Most schools in the early years were affiliated with or held in local churches or sponsored by the community in which they were located. (LCPL.)

This undated photograph of Bethany Church School shows students from many grades. This school was supported by Bethany United Methodist Church in the northeastern part of the county. (LCPL.)

Double Branches School is shown with students from all grades in 1924. There are too many to name, but the teachers in the back row are, from left or right, Tommie Beggs and Haynie Prince. (Courtesy of Jeannette Moragne.)

Four Points School students from the middle school grades pose for this shot in 1928. The teacher, Marie Albea, sits directly in the middle. The school was located near Tankersley's Store at the crossroads of Double Branches Road and US 220. (LCPL.)

GOLD MINE SCHOOL PUPILS - 1891

Gold Mine School in 1891 was located in the northwestern part of the county. The teacher was Lessie Standard Lowe. This might have been near the Sale Gold Mine. (LCPL.)

Students at Graves Mountain School pose for this picture in 1919. The teacher's name is J.T. Hudson. This was one of the community schools located in the western part of Lincoln County, not far from the Wilkes County line. Those children who lived on or near Graves Mountain would have attended this school, which taught all grades. (LCPL.)

Students of Lafayette School pose in 1928, with teachers Ida Morrison and Clyde Bentley in the center. This school was located on Lewis-Crook Road in the western part of the county. (LCPL.)

Liberty Hill School in 1908 has students of all ages, taught by Prof. Welcome Smalley (far right). It was located in the southeastern part of the county. (LCPL.)

Liberty Hill School students pose with teacher Myrtis Gunby (far left) around 1919. (LCPL.)

Lincolnton School elementary students were photographed in the 1940–1941 school year. (LCPL.)

Here are some middle school students at Lincolnton School during 1953–1954. Prior to the unification of local schools, the Lincolnton School served those children living within the city limits for the most part. Most Lincoln County children outside the city limits attended their community schools. (LCPL.)

Professor Body, shown in the center of the back row, taught Loco School in the early 1900s. (Courtesy of Dot Scott.)

Loco School in 1916 had these students enrolled with teacher Orie Smalley. (LCPL.)

Loco Church Music School was an annual training school. This photograph was taken of the students in 1919. It was supported by Loco Baptist Church. (Courtesy of Bobby Aycock.)

Midway School in the Midway community shows a thriving student body, with too many pupils to name, in 1911. The teacher on the far right is Pearl Kirkland Norman. (LCPL.)

This photograph of these unidentified people includes the Midway School in the background. The school was supported by the Midway United Methodist Church and was located in the northern part of the county. The building was later destroyed. (LCPL.)

New Hope School students sit for this photograph in 1913, with teacher Ethel Ward wearing the hat. The New Hope Baptist Church supported this school, located in southern Lincoln County near Cliatt's Corner, at US 220 and Augusta Highway. (LCPL.)

Salem School, built in 1911, is now located in the Lincoln County Historical Park. It was affiliated with Salem Baptist Church and was donated to the Lincoln County Historical Society as an example of the one-room schoolhouse. During the annual Pioneer Day in November at the park, speakers give lectures on various topics in the schoolhouse. (LCPL.)

Smith Chapel School, known as "Sweet Easy," was once an active school for the black community. The sign over the door shows a "going-to-church" scene on the left and a "classroom" scene on the right. It has fallen into disuse and disrepair today. (Photograph by Mitchum.)

This is the last field trip of Westside High School, class of 1969. In 1970, the students were integrated into Lincoln County High School, formerly known as Lincolnton High School. In the back row, the men with hats are teachers Willie James Harris (left) and Alexander Burch Mason. The two women directly in front of them are teachers Annie H. Patterson and Shirley Byrd. (LCPL.)

The Lincoln County High School building served as the primary site for high school activities until 2010, when the new high school was dedicated. (LCPL.)

Lincolnton High School friends
in 1923 are seen posing on the
steps of the school or hanging
out the window. (Courtesy
of Jeannette Moragne.)

Betty Ivey (left) and Marifaith
Teasley are seen enjoying the grass
at Lincolnton High School in
1947. (Courtesy of Lilly Turner.)

Members of the Lincolnton High School Library Club stand or kneel outside the high school building in 1953–1954. Club members usually helped the school librarian with shelving and other duties. (Courtesy of Jeannette Moragne.)

Lincolnton School's "Green Building," built in 1920, is seen behind Christina Probst. The Green Building, located at the corner of Sunrise Drive and Dallas Street, burned in 1971. This location is now the site of the Title I Administration Building of the Lincoln County Board of Education erected in 1971. One can almost see the footprint of the original building at the site. (LCPL.)

The number of students graduating in Lincoln County High School's class of 1997 shows the growth of the school system. (LCPL.)

These Lincolnton schoolchildren are like many other groups of students throughout the years. Although the date for this photograph is unknown, what makes it interesting is the man peering over the fence (on the right), who appears to have on some type of military or postal service hat. (LCPL.)

William Henry Spires Jr., celebrating his 94th birthday, demonstrates the die-hard nature of Lincolnton/Lincoln County High School graduates and their love for their Red Devils' football and other sports teams. (Courtesy of Mamie Neil Reed.)

Six

CHURCHES

N.C. and Matilda Ware, Joseph B. and Margaret Ware, Nancy Murray, Jane E. Richardson, and Lemuel Wynn and his wife organized Anthony Chapel United Methodist Church in 1848. (Photograph by Mitchum.)

Beulah Baptist Church was founded in 1807 but was called "Union" because it shared a meetinghouse with Methodists and Presbyterians. A vote to change to the current name occurred in 1854 after the church moved to its current location. The building had to be rebuilt several times due to storm or other damage, but the congregation had its bicentennial on August 12, 2007. (Photograph by Mitchum.)

New Hope Baptist Church began as a brush arbor congregation in 1829 near its present site and organized in 1830. It was known as "Old Field Church," "Old Hope," "Poor Hope," and finally, "New Hope." (Photograph by Mitchum.)

Double Branches Baptist Church was established prior to 1803, originally as a meeting place for Baptists, Methodists, and Presbyterians, who often shared preachers. In 1830, fourteen members were dismissed to become charter members of New Hope Baptist Church. (LCPL.)

The growth of Double Branches Baptist Church can be seen in the church buildings today. (Photograph by Mitchum.)

This photograph, although not sharp, shows Ebenezer Baptist Church at the funeral of Rev. William Thomas Mason in April 1960. His handwritten history of Ebenezer Baptist Church in 1947 states the following: "[It] had its beginning as most churches in the deep south assembled with the Christians of the white church. To benefit both races the pulpit was located near the center of the church where each could hear the rich word as was delivered by the earnest minister (white)." (LCPL.)

Today, Ebenezer Baptist Church shows what Reverend Mason stated at the end of his history of the church, "Lives of great men all remind us we can make our lives sublime and departing leave behind us footprints on the sands of time." Reverend Mason certainly left his footprints on the sands of Ebenezer Baptist Church. (Photograph by Mitchum.)

First Assembly Church of God was established recently and is a Protestant religious organization. Its programs include Kingdom Kidz, Royal Rangers, Mpact girls' clubs, and a sports ministry called Upward. It is one of the fastest-growing churches in the county. (Photograph by Mitchum.)

Goshen Baptist Church was organized in 1787 and was the first Baptist church in Lincoln County. Originally it was named Rocky Spring, but its name changed to Goshen in 1817. It, too, shared facilities with Baptists, Methodists, and Presbyterians. Methodist bishop Francis Asbury mentions the new chapel in the area, which is likely the old facility. In 1835, the Baptists built their own building, which is now the main auditorium of the present church. (Photograph by Mitchum.)

Greenwood Baptist Church, established in 1784 as Upton Creek Baptist Church, was moved and renamed in 1788. The final move to Lincoln County occurred in 1812, and the present meetinghouse was completed in 1816. As part of their missionary tenets, members organized Lincolnton Baptist Church in 1825 and Salem Baptist Church in 1827. (Photograph by Mitchum.)

This aerial view shows Harmony Baptist Church, established in 1874 by the following seven members: Eliza Zellars, Emma Blackburn, Arline Dallas, and Rachel Harmon and Richard Hardmon, Joseph Tucker, and John Zellars. The church school closed at the end of the 1953–1954 school year. (LCPL.)

Hephzibah Baptist Church was formed in 1831 and had a school connected to the church somewhere on the grounds; however, the school is seldom mentioned in church records. This is likely a photograph taken before 1900 of the old church building that was sold after the new church was completed and dedicated in 1912. (LCPL.)

This is the modern Hephzibah Baptist Church, with the building completed in 1912 and additions made in subsequent years. (Photograph by Mitchum.)

Lincolnton Baptist Church was one of the churches established by the Greenwood Baptist Church in 1825 as the Old Union Meetinghouse. Due to disagreements, members left and formed the Siloam Baptist Church in 1876. The old Lincolnton Baptist Church was dissolved in 1880, and in 1883, the Siloam congregation changed its name back to Lincolnton Baptist Church. The new church was finished in 1921. An education building was added in 1955 and a fellowship hall in 1971. (Photograph by Mitchum.)

Lincolnton Presbyterian Church was established in 1823 and still meets in the building that once was called the Old Union Meetinghouse. This photograph was taken in July 1938; the building has changed little today, except for new windows, vinyl siding, and a small roof over the front steps. (LCPL.)

Lincolnton United Methodist Church was organized in the first quarter of the 1800s. Historians who have written about Lincoln County say, "Colonel Peter Lamar of Lincolnton donated a tract of land in Lincolnton upon which a house of worship was built." From 1912 to 1915, a building was erected, originally as a wooden structure with a bell tower on the right corner and the first stained-glass windows in the county. The Sunday school building was added in 1950, and the social hall was built in 1960. (Photograph by Mitchum.)

In 1895, members of Greenwood, Hephzibah, and Salem churches met to constitute a church at Wheat Campground. The building was dedicated in 1897 as Loco Baptist Church. Loco, it should be noted, is a place, not a state of mind. (Photograph by Mitchum.)

St. Paul United Methodist Church has one of the oldest cemeteries in the county, with the graves of Hezekiah Bussey and Zachariah Spires, who fought in the Revolutionary War. (Photograph by Mitchum.)

Midway United Methodist Church, organized in 1906, was located between the communities of Goshen and Chennault and started gathering in homes as brush arbor meetings. The building was completed in 1907, with the porch and columns added in 1967 and the steeple added in 1978. (Photograph by Mitchum.)

Martin's Crossroads Congregational Holiness Church was established in the late 20th century at the corner of US 220 and Double Branches Road. It has experienced steady growth in membership. (Photograph by Mitchum.)

Morningside Baptist Church was established in 1983 by former members of Lincolnton Baptist Church and others. The current building was erected in 1987 on Elm Street. (Photograph by Mitchum.)

The following is from Mount Zion Baptist Church history: "In 1868, the white brethren of the Salem Baptist Church requested the colored brethren to see if they could get Reverend E.V. White to preach for one Sunday each month." This is an offspring of Salem Baptist Church and is "the oldest Negro church in the county," organized in 1871. The first building was erected in 1883 but destroyed by fire in 1977; a new church was built. (Photograph by Mitchum.)

Mulberry United Methodist Church was established in 1873. There is an old school building in the woods behind the church. (Photograph by Mitchum.)

Newberry Missionary Baptist Church was organized in 1873 by the "white brethren of Double Branches Baptist Church." It was located one mile from its present location. It was moved in 1948 because of the construction of the Clarks Hill Dam and lake at Clarks Hill, South Carolina. Although this is the original building constructed in 1907, many renovations have taken place. (LCPL.)

Newberry Missionary Baptist Church, as it looks today, shows the renovations made to the original building. (Photograph by Mitchum.)

Bethany United Methodist Church was established before 1898, but little can be found about its history. It is the sister church, since 1976, to one of the oldest in the county, Pine Grove United Methodist Church. (Photograph by Mitchum.)

The oldest existing Methodist church in Lincoln County is Pine Grove United Methodist Church. It started as a brush arbor meeting until the log building was built in 1806. It has the oldest continuous Sunday school to present time. The current church shows the renovations from 1964, stained-glass windows added in 1969, and brick veneer added in 1973. (Photograph by Mitchum.)

Seven

QUALITY OF LIFE

Jerry Hammie Ashmore's 350-acre farm was located in the Double Branches community. He was a sharecropper farmer who owned and operated a feed-and-seed store specializing in fertilizer. He is sitting in his 1912 Metz, only the second car in the county. Henrietta "Mammy" Percival Ashmore stands to the far right on the front porch of the house. The other people have not been identified. (LCPL.)

The original Crawford Drugstore on Peachtree Street in Lincolnton is shown in 1918. Standing on the left is pharmacist Elam Guillebeau, with proprietor Dr. William Beall Crawford, and William B. Crawford Jr. seated at a table. (Courtesy of Eddy Turner.)

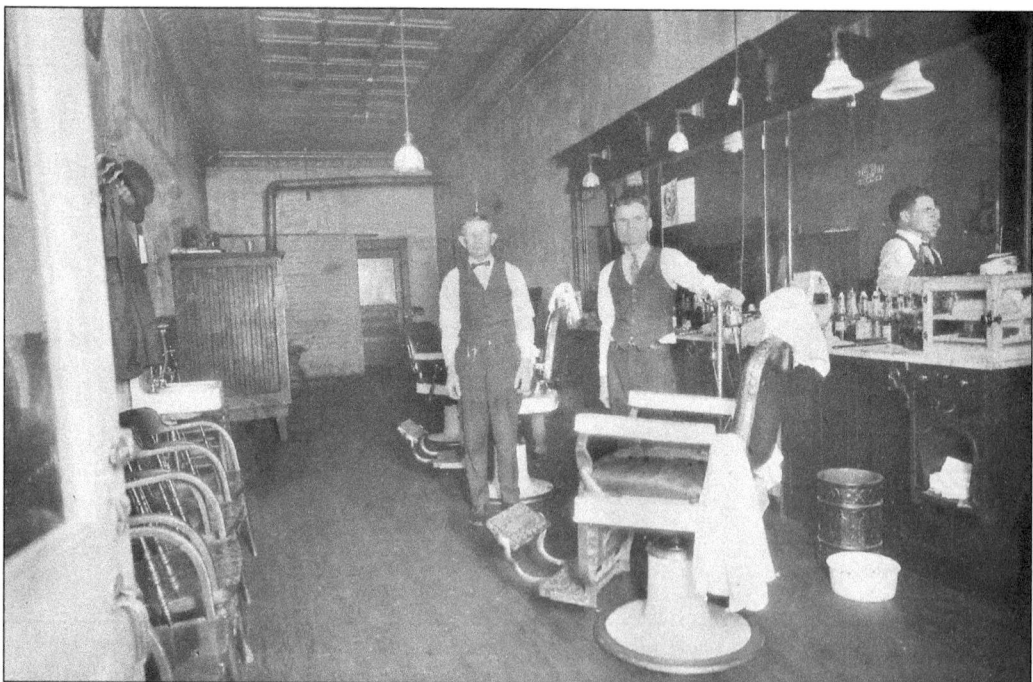

Found on Peachtree Street, this barbershop was located in one of the earliest brick buildings in Lincolnton in 1919. The people in the photograph are unidentified. (Courtesy of Laura Spratlin.)

Groves Store was owned by Cooksey Lucius "C.L." Groves and W.H. Groves. They built and operated this store at the corner of Peachtree Street and Ward Avenue into the 20th century. Other owners over the years included W.N. Albea, J.R. Smalley, Manly Deason, and finally, Jimmy Deason. (LCPL.)

The first courthouse built in Lincolnton sat at the town square on Washington Street, now the site of the Confederate monument. This photograph shows the second courthouse, built in 1874 for $12,000 and used until 1915. (LCPL.)

Men worked on the clock tower of the new courthouse in 1915. Almost 100 years later, the clock still keeps perfect time! (Courtesy of Kenneth Adair.)

The current courthouse in Lincolnton was built in 1915. Willis Irvin Sr., one of the leading architects in Augusta, Georgia, designed it. (Photograph by Mitchum.)

Aycock service station was located at the corner of Elm and Peachtree Streets at the site now known as Wayne Epp's Dixie Quick. (Courtesy of Bobby Aycock.)

Jimmy Deason's Grocery and Feed store began its existence as Groves Store. It was located next to the Groves-May house. When that house was moved to the Lincoln County Historical Park, the water tower and Deason's store were removed to make way for Bell's Grocery store and parking lot. (Courtesy of Eddy Turner.)

Norman Brothers Grocery Store, built by Billy Norman and Murray Toombs Norman, was located somewhere in Lincoln County. Standing on the porch are, from left to right, Barbara Guthrie Gibbs, Gail Guthrie Remsen, Marianne Myers Adams, Ronnie Myers, and Ernie Guthrie. Norma Myers Turner is off the porch. (LCPL.)

Peyton Wyatt "P.W." Norman's store was located on Highway 378 near the Wilkes County line. Most people called it "Mae Sallie's," because of the work and efforts of his wife. The two gentlemen shown in this photograph are unidentified. (LCPL.)

Joe Holloway (seated) is in his store, which was located in the Double Branches community. Larry Goolsby, his grandson, peeks out from behind his chair in 1957. (Courtesy of Jeannette Moragne.)

This building in the Double Branches community originally housed C.M. May's store, which was bought by John Marshall Price. He was made postmaster of Double Branches with the post office in the store. Until it closed in 1996, it was one of the oldest authentic general stores still in operation in Georgia. Other owners of the store were Theron Price, Billy and Inez McWhorter, Jane and Fred McWhorter, and currently, Mike Reese. (Photograph by Mitchum.)

The Keeter Building is at the corner of Washington Street and Metasville Road. It was erected in the early 1920s by Charlie Keeter. One can see the spare tire on the rear of a car in the window on the left, so this photograph was probably taken when that space was used for selling vehicles in the early 20th century. (LCPL.)

Men are spending quality time in front of Spratlin's store sometime before 1940. (Courtesy of Laura Spratlin.)

Maurice and Cehoy McDaniel Spires dress up for an Old-Fashioned Day at Bethany Church in 1962. They make a perfect pioneer couple. (Courtesy of Maurice Spires.)

Lovelace Hotel, in the Lovelace community, was situated at a stop on the Washington & Lincolnton Railroad that operated from 1918 to 1932. When the line was completed from Washington to Lovelace, citizens celebrated, although it was just one mile into Lincoln County. (LCPL.)

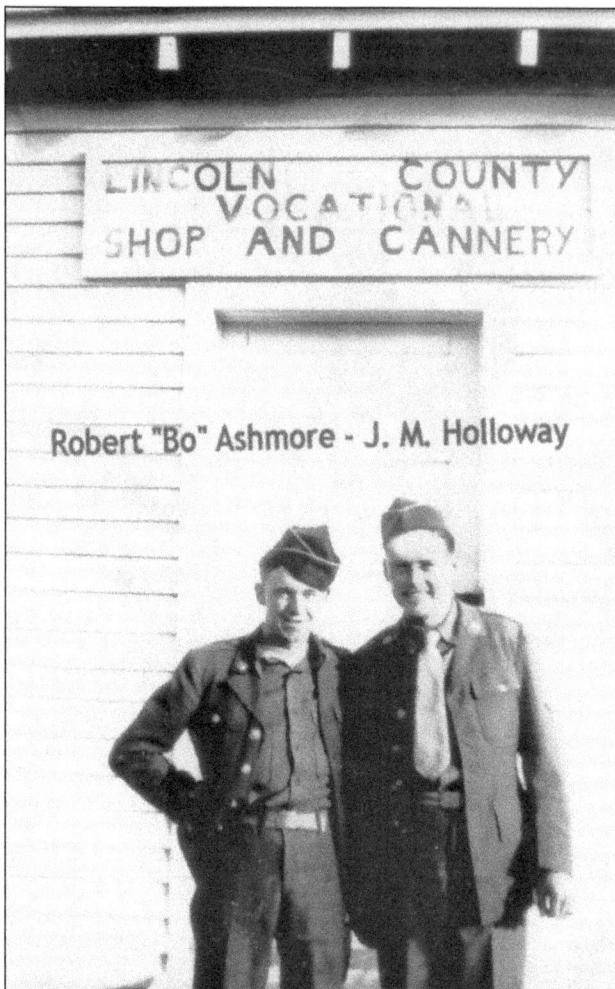

Robert "Bo" Ashmore (left) and J.M. Holloway stand in front of the Lincoln County Vocational Shop and Cannery, located on Sunrise Drive near the Green Building, during the 1940s. (Courtesy of Jeannette Moragne.)

There is no date on this photograph of the post office, and those who are familiar with Lincolnton's postal service think it might have been the second of four sites for the post office in Lincolnton. This building was located at the corner of Main and Washington Streets. Many of the other communities in Lincoln County had their own post offices until they were consolidated into the Lincolnton office. (LCPL.)

In their cotton field, Ellis Holloway and family members take a break and drink their Pepsi-Colas. From left to right are an unidentified man, Herman, Carrie Lou, and Ellis Holloway. (Courtesy of Lilly Turner.)

Hubert Nash dresses a hog while his wife, Violet, and son Morgan watch. (Courtesy of Jackie Willingham.)

During Prohibition, there was a thriving business in the county—bootlegging. The newspaper reported many stills that were destroyed. Here is the evidence of the haul from one of those raids with Sheriff Wiley S. Harrison, who is probably the man wearing the three-piece suit in the middle of the photograph. Harrison was sheriff from 1921–1924. (LCPL.)

Despite the law, young men such as George Turner (left) and Grover Cleveland Harrison could be found imbibing whenever possible. This photograph was taken before 1930. (LCPL.)

Pal the cow lived within the city limits of Lincolnton in the field behind the houses on Peachtree Street. The house on the left was a private residence that was converted to apartments. In the distance on the right is the steeple of the Lincolnton Baptist Church. (Courtesy of Jackie Willingham.)

As one regional mechanic stated, "If you were in the car business, you knew you had to deal with Minnie Wells and the Wells Oil Company in Lincolnton." This building on the Augusta Highway now houses several companies but was once all part of the Wells Oil Company. (LCPL.)

This building on the main thoroughfare of Lincolnton houses the *Lincoln Journal*, the newspaper serving the county. (Courtesy of Jackie Willingham.)

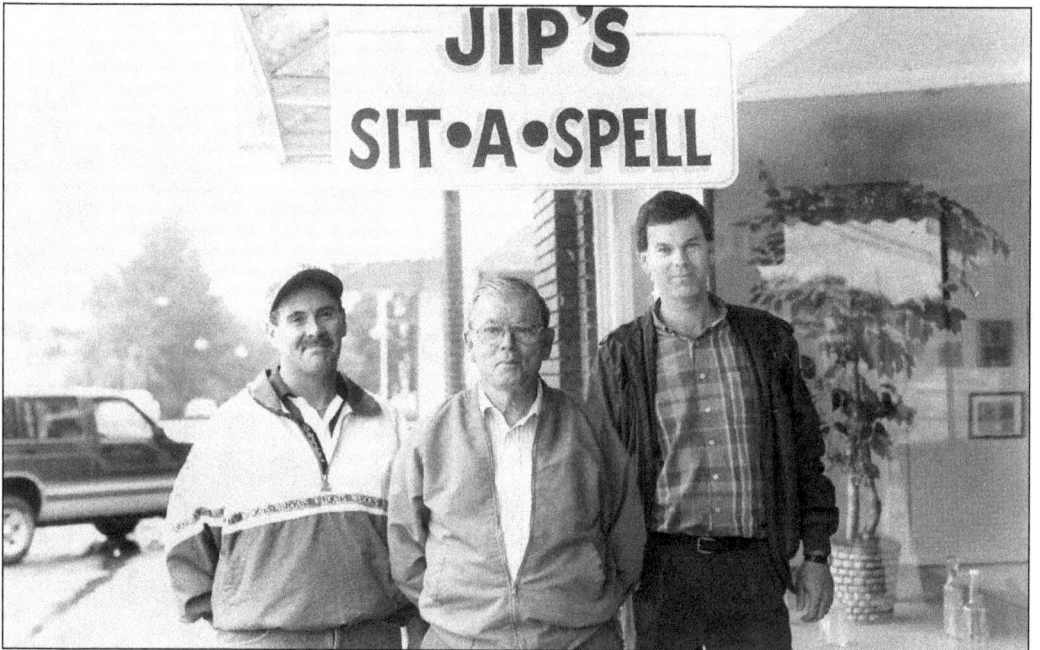

Jip's Sit-A-Spell was a unique place in the county. Jip Smalley (center) opened the space for retired men to come, sit, talk, reminisce, and spend time. There was no admission, nothing to buy, and nothing for sale. It opened in 1993 and closed after his death in 2001. (LCPL.)

Eight

OTHER PEOPLE
AND PLACES

Wyatt None Albea and wife, Lillian
Alethia Groves, owners of the W.N. Albea
General Merchandise store, pose for this
photograph with son Wyatt Bernard
around 1912. (Courtesy of Nina Albea.)

The Guillebeau family stands on the steps of the Guillebeau Hotel sometime between 1950 and 1972. (Courtesy of Nina Albea.)

This is a portrait of the Mary Brown Guillebeau family. The date is unknown. (LCPL.)

This bluegrass band from the Loco community plays in the late 1930s. The band members are, from left to right, Raleigh Long, Romulus Long, James C. Justice, Bill Long, Joe Strother, Ed Graves, and Al Jones. The members of this band taught the original Lewis Family Band. (LCPL.)

The Lewis family, "America's First Family of Bluegrass Gospel," started touring regularly in the 1960s and continued touring until 2010. Several generations of family members entered the group as time passed. They were inducted into the Georgia Music Hall of Fame in 1992 and the International Bluegrass Music Hall of Honor in 2006. Carrying on the legacy is the Little Roy and Lizzy Show, with Little Roy Lewis and Lizzy Long. (Courtesy of Jeannette Moragne.)

This photograph of the Freeman girls was taken around 1925. On the left is Alma Freeman Williams, and on the right is Doris Freeman Gunby. The child in the middle is unidentified. (LCPL.)

Here is an undated photograph of the Hardy family, known to be residents of Lincoln County. (LCPL.)

The Hogan family poses for a family picture. It, too, was taken at an unknown time during the 20th century. (Courtesy of Mary Stidom Hogan.)

A different Hogan family has a reunion; the date is unknown but probably in the early 20th century. (LCPL.)

This photograph shows Morgan Henry Holloway II family members at their home in the Double Branches community around 1915. From left to right are Fannie Forrest Reese (wife), Frances Minerva (Bohler), Joseph Miller, and Nettie (Paradise). (Courtesy of Jeannette Moragne.)

A portable sawmill is shown with Mitchell Ivey reclining in the front right. The sawmills were taken to the trees, rather than trucking the trees to the sawmill. This photograph was probably taken in the 1930s. (Courtesy of Lilly Turner.)

Jesse Maddox (1895–1957) stands, holding his grandchild, in front of his barn. The date of this photograph is unknown. (Courtesy of Dale Maddox.)

Jefferson Davis Martin is shown sometime around 1900 with his wife, Annie Julia Dunaway (seated), and children, from left to right, Orlena, Roy, and Bonnie. Unfortunately, one son, Freddie, died when he was four years old, before this photograph was taken. (LCPL.)

Lucy Martin (left), Toombs Adolphus Norman, and Ella Martin are prepared to go to the fair in Washington, Georgia, in October 1913. (Courtesy of Billy Norman.)

Sam and Julie McMahan (seated, center front) and family relax on their front porch; the date is unknown. (Courtesy of Lamar McKinney.)

The Norman family home place was on Prater Road. Pictured in the foreground are, from left to right, John Lewis, Walter, Addie Massie, Thomas Adiel Norman holding Jack, Mary Lou Cullars Norman, Lalla Bell, Cluese, Lenoir, Toombs Adolphus, and Maude, along with unidentified household workers in back. This photograph was taken in the 1890s. (Billy Norman.)

Will and Kate C. Norman pose with their children, from left to right, Essie, Bessie, Mabel, Ralph, Lonnie, Peyton, and Frank. (LCPL.)

Edward (left) and Robert Reid pose for this portrait in the mid- to late 1940s. Older brother Hubert had a portrait made at the same time, but it is not included here. (Courtesy of Maggie Stidom Hogan.)

Gladys (left) and Irene Reid also had their portrait made, apparently at the same time as their brothers. (Courtesy of Maggie Stidom Hogan.)

The Thomas Jackson and Mary Elizabeth "Molly" Downer Scott family is at their home place in 1908. On the left is Millie Agather Bullard Hudson Downer (Mitt), and on the right are the seven surviving children. The children's names are (eldest to youngest) Margaret Estelle, Thomas Eugene Watson, Millie Wakefield, William Jackson, Roselyn Reba, Stuart Humphrey, and Christopher McCoy Scott Sr. (Courtesy of Dot Scott.)

The children of "Jennie Mama" (Elizabeth Jane) and "Frank Papa" (Frank Lindsey) Scott are, from left to right, (first row) Janie Gertrude Scott Henderson, Nobie Henry Scott Norman, Woottie Callaway Scott Dye Ware, Leila Frances Scott Parks, and Mary Elizabeth "Lizzie" Scott Sprouse; (second row) Lucy Finelle Scott Hopkins, John Haynes Scott, George Walton Scott, Gracie Scott Drinkard, and Sarah Wakefield Scott Lindsey. Clara Evilena Scott Chapman was absent when this photograph was made. (Courtesy of Dot Scott.)

Willie Bell Turner holds her daughter Brenda Turner (Danner-McGahee), who would one day become the tax commissioner for Lincoln County. (Courtesy of Brenda Danner-McGahee.)

The Ware family is one of the first families of Lincoln County. There have been Wares since the beginning of the county, and they were known for their appreciation of a good education. These Ware children, descended from Robert A. Ware, pose for this picture sometime in the 1960s. (LCPL.)

Edward Denwead Gassaway sits in his car while Pete (left) and Hayes Bohler pose for the photographer in the early 1910s. (Courtesy of Jeannette Moragne.)

From left to right, Violet and Louise Banks, Betty and Dorothy Turner, and Mary Saggus relax at the Clyde Ivey home place in the Iveytown community in the 1940s. (Courtesy of Lilly Turner.)

This Drinkard home place photograph was taken in 1920, with mother Blanche (in the white dress) and baby Helen (in chair); the others are unidentified. The home place is located at the end of Humphrey Street. (LCPL.)

This c. 1915 photograph of the Tullis family home place has the family posing in front. Pictured are, from left to right, William Davis (son), Dolly the mule, Millard Carey (son), John Calvin (father), Frances Mae (daughter), Frances Emma Griffin (mother), Maggie Allene (daughter), and Walter Lawton (behind mule, probably a relative of John Calvin's mother, who was a Lawton). The house was torn down on October 31, 1999. (Courtesy of Dot Scott.)

M. Holliday (left) and Lillian Georgia "L.G." Dozier wrote on the back of this photograph, "Sweet Sixteen and never been kissed by nobody—yet." L.G. was the daughter of the Dozier Hotel owners, Lovick L. and Lillie Bell Hogan Dozier. She married Hugh Green and lived in the first brick house built in Lincoln County. "Miss L.G." was beloved by the community. (LCPL.)

Thomas Watson Wellmaker (left) and Tom Crook pose for the camera in 1920s. (Courtesy of Dot Scott.)

Thomas Adiel Norman (seated) and Will Henderson pose for this portrait around 1890. (Courtesy of Billy Norman.)

Alvin and Betty Willingham pose with their son Clyde. No further information is available. (Courtesy of Jackie Willingham.)

A family reunion photograph shows the Simmons family. The gentleman wearing the hat is Plott Simmons, and his wife, Marie Bennett Simmons, is on his left. Others include Clara Simmons Beard (third row, fourth from left), Yolanda Beard (first row, first on left), Angel Beard (first row, third from left), Carol Dean Henderson (third row, first on right), George Anne Freeman (fifth row, first on left), George Simmons (third row, second from right), Ella Simmons (behind Plott's right shoulder), and Minnie Simmons (behind George, on his right). (LCPL.)

The children of Moseley Hawes and Sarah Elizabeth "Bessie" Norman Wright pose for a reunion photograph. They include Ruth Irene, Moody Lenwood, Clyde Watson, Thomas Blanchard, Guy Hawes, Ida Mae, Rebecca, Norman Alexander, and Lottie Allene. (Courtesy of Jacqueline Johnson.)

Thomas Clayton Fleming and Mary Elizabeth Spires enjoy each other's company in the mid-1940s. They were married on October 25, 1949. (Courtesy of Mamie Neil Reed.)

John Hogan Bentley (1869–1939) and Mary Elizabeth "Lizzie" Graves Bentley (1872–1947) stand in front of a car at their home near the Agnes community. (Courtesy of Edwin Bentley.)

Louis Aycock and Sudie Chamberlain Sims outside Sims Store in the 1970s. "Miss Sudie" (1888–1986) was known and loved by all who met her and was devoted to Pine Grove United Methodist Church, where she served as a Sunday school teacher for over 50 years. (Courtesy of Virginia Aycock.)

Each year, Jip Smalley, who owned a furniture store, would hold a raffle at Christmastime and give tickets to all residents of the county. If ticket holders were there and their number was called, they could win anything from couches to refrigerators. This picture was probably taken during the late 20th century. (LCPL.)

These young people are in costume for some occasion. They are in the garden of the Dozier Hotel, which was once a mansion that was converted to a hotel in the late 1800s. The hotel burned to the ground in the early 1920s. To the left in the background are the steeples of Lincolnton United Methodist Church. (LCPL.)

Iris Nash Sale became clerk of Lincoln County Superior Court in 1956 and held the office for 16 years. She was deputy clerk under Wilburn Tutt Dunaway for 21 years prior to being elected. Sale died at the age of 87 in 1992. Here, she is at work in her office at the courthouse. (LCPL.)

Essie Mae Ross Cartledge is on duty at the Loco Telephone switchboard for the last time. This was the last local community-owned telephone exchange until it merged with Wilkes Telephone and Electric Company, which is currently the only local landline telephone service provider. (LCPL.)

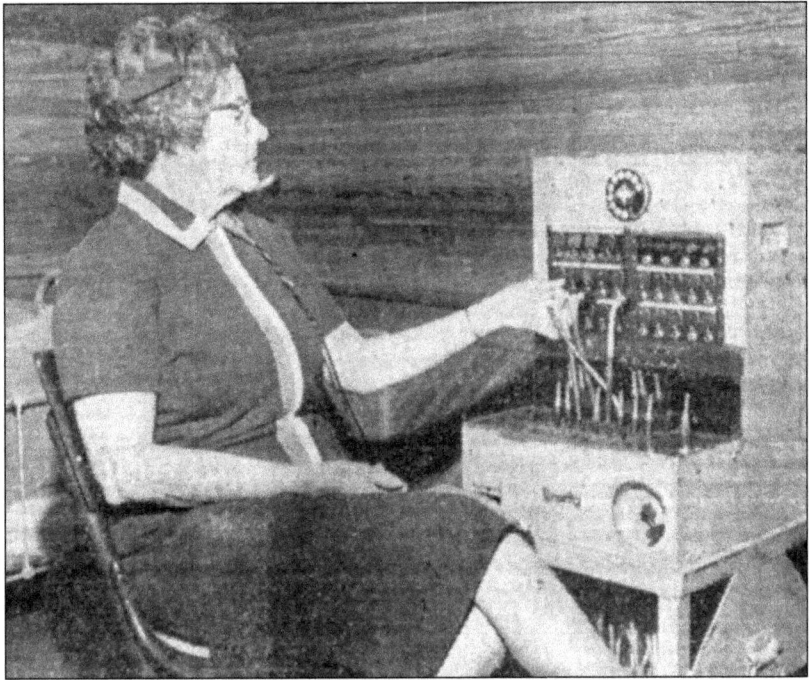

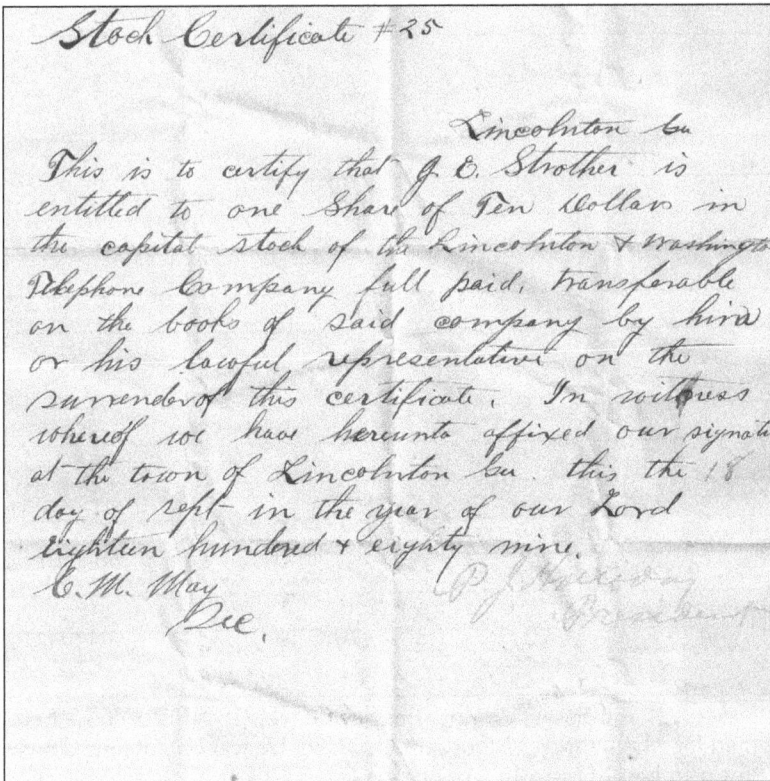

This Lincolnton and Washington Telephone Company stock certificate was issued to J.E. Strother on September 18, 1889, and signed by C.M. May. Strother bought one share of stock for $10. May was also the manager of the Coca-Cola Bottling Company, shown on the cover. (Courtesy of Dianne M. Poteat.)

This photograph of the home place of Nathaniel C. and Mary E. Bussey Moss was taken in the early 20th century. With a porch in the front, this residence is typical of the style of houses built in the county. (Courtesy of Jeannette Moragne.)

Robert Newton Graves (1843–1922) and Susan Virginia Bentley Graves (1849–1919) pose here. Robert is a relative of the man for whom Graves Mountain is named. He was one of four Graves brothers who were important members of Lincoln County society. (LCPL.)

In this 1899 letter from Otis Ashmore (1852–1934) to his nephew Otis Partridge, Ashmore writes about visiting Lincolnton, traveling via train. Ashmore is renown as an educator and author of the astronomical section of *Grier's Almanac*, which was first published in 1807 and is still in publication. Ashmore lived and worked in Savannah, Georgia. His family and relatives remained in Lincoln County, and he visited regularly. (Courtesy of Dianne M. Poteat.)

Members of the Washington & Lincolnton Railroad Board of Directors stand in front of the "bus" that carried passengers on the line between Lincolnton and Washington in 1920. Standing are, from left to right, Holcomb (manager of railroad), Lloyd Johnson, R.F. Guillebeau, Rocheford Johnson, two unidentified people, O.B. Wright, Chennault, unidentified, J.J. Glaze, Ed Deason, unidentified, R.E. Crawford, unidentified, Roy Groves, and Jim Sturkey. In the doorway are Wilson McKinney (left) and Tom Hardy. (LCPL.)

Visit us at
arcadiapublishing.com